DISCOVER

ANCIENT

CHINA

DISCOVER
ANCIENT
CHINA

Neil D. Bramwell

Enslow Publishers, Inc.
40 Industrial Road
Box 398
Berkeley Heights, NJ 07922
USA
http://www.enslow.com

Ancient China

18th Century B.C. — A.D. 5th Century

Gobi Desert

CHINA

= Shang Dynasty c. 1523–1027 B.C.

= Qin Dynasty 221 B.C.–207 B.C.

= Han Dynasty 206 B.C.– A.D. 220

------- Current borders of China

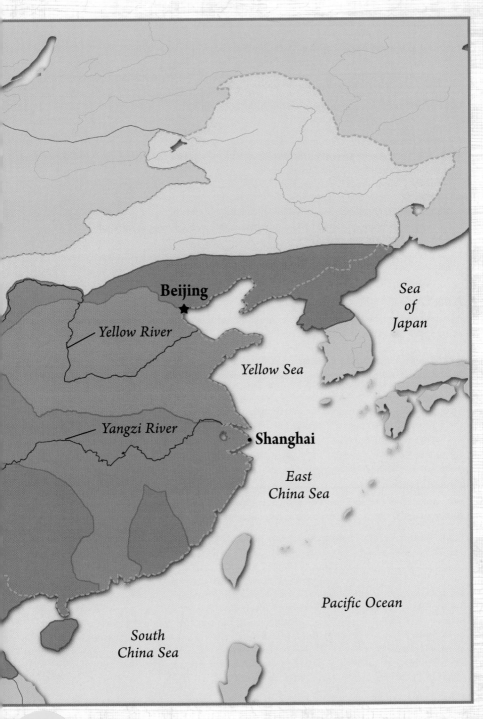

Beijing

Yellow River

Yangzi River

• Shanghai

Sea
of
Japan

Yellow Sea

East
China Sea

Pacific Ocean

South
China Sea

This book originally published as *Ancient China* in 2004.

Library of Congress Cataloging-in-Publication Data

Bramwell, Neil D., 1932-
  Discover ancient China / Neil D. Bramwell.
    p. cm. — (Discover ancient civilizations)
  Includes bibliographical references and index.
  Summary: "Learn about the art and cultural contributions, family life, religions and people of ancient China"—Provided by publisher.
  ISBN 978-0-7660-4194-3
  1. China—Civilization—To 221 B.C.—Juvenile literature. 2. China—Civilization—221 B.C.-960 A.D.—Juvenile literature. I. Title.
  DS741.65.B73 2012
  931—dc23

                                              2012011570

Future editions:
Paperback ISBN: 978-1-4644-0331-6   EPUB ISBN: 978-1-4645-1185-1
Single-User PDF ISBN: 978-1-4646-1185-8   Multi-User PDF ISBN: 978-0-7660-5814-9

Printed in the United States of America
112013 Lake Book Manufacturing, Inc., Melrose Park, IL
10 9 8 7 6 5 4 3 2 1

To Our Readers: We have done our best to make sure all Internet Addresses in this book were active and appropriate when we went to press. However, the author and the publisher have no control over and assume no liability for the material available on those Internet sites or on other Web sites they may link to. Any comments or suggestions can be sent by e-mail to comments@enslow.com or to the address on the back cover

♻ Enslow Publishers, Inc., is committed to printing our books on recycled paper. The paper in every book contains 10% to 30% post-consumer waste (PCW). The cover board on the outside of each book contains 100% PCW. Our goal is to do our part to help young people and the environment too!

Photo Credits: ©2012 Photos.com, a division of Getty Images. All rights reserved., pp. 26-27, 54, 61, 63; ©1998-2004, TravelChinaGuide.com, pp. 22, 24; ©AP Photos/Anat Givon, p. 77; ©AP Photos/Huang jundong sx—Imaginechina, p. 74; ©AP Photos/Xia yu gz—Imaginechina, p. 73; ©Clipart.com/©2012 Photos.com, a division of Getty Images. All rights reserved., p. 32(bottom), 50, 76, 83; ©Corel Corporation, pp. 32(top), 42-43, 66-67; ©Enslow Publishers, Inc, p. 20; China National Tourism Administration, p. 90; Courtesy of Government Printing Office, Republic of China, p. 78; hanhanpeggy/©2012 Photos.com, a division of Getty Images., pp. 86-87; Hemera Photo Objects, p. 79; Holger Mette /© 2012 Photos.com, a division of Getty Images. All rights reserved., pp. 12-13, HU-JUN/©2012 Photos.com, a division of Getty Images. All rights reserved., pp. 34-35; Inna Felker /© 2012 Photos.com, a division of Getty Images. All rights reserved., p. 18; Kristin McCarthy/©Enslow Publishers, Inc, pp. 4-5; Shutterstock, pp. 75, 88, 92

Cover Photo Credits: Great Wall: ©2012 Photos.com, a division of Getty Images. All rights reserved.;Terra-cotta warrior: Shutterstock

Table of
CONTENTS

Chapter 1

An ARMY PROTECTS the FIRST EMPEROR

In Xi'an, a city in the Shaanxi province of northwestern China, thousands of soldiers, perhaps more than seven thousand, stand in formation in three underground pits. They are ready to defend their emperor, whose body lies entombed nearby, from any enemy. They have remained in formation, ready for battle, for over two thousand years. The soldiers are 8 inches to 6 feet 2.5 inches tall, and are made of terra-cotta, a form of baked clay. Each soldier's features are unique to him. Their weapons, longbows, spears, battle-axes, and halberds, which combine a spear and a battle-ax, are stored nearby. These soldiers are known as the terra-cotta warriors, and the 14,000-square-foot museum where they reside is one of China's most-visited cultural sites.

The soldiers are arrayed in formations according to their function in battle, ready to ward off attackers from any direction. Some soldiers are in kneeling positions while others are standing. There are also seventy-four full-size chariots, drawn by four horses each, in which other soldiers or officers ride. There are, as well, nearly six hundred life-size Mongolian ponies.

Each soldier wears a uniform whose color corresponds to his rank. The colors are purple, blue, green, yellow, red, and orange. The uniforms range from heavy knee-length tunics and cloth leg wrappings to armor made from hundreds of pieces of iron shaped like fish scales.[1]

The emperor's tomb that these soldiers have been guarding for over two thousand years took over thirty years to build and is located west of the burial chambers of the army. The tomb itself has not yet been excavated, but according to legend, it is supposed to be a replica of his empire, with rivers of quicksilver (mercury) and many marvels, including death traps for any tomb robbers.[2]

The terra-cotta warriors who have been guarding the tomb of Emperor Shi Huangdi were discovered in 1974 by Chinese farmers who were drilling a well.

Shi Huangdi (Qin Shi Huang), the emperor who had this army buried to protect himself for all time, founded the first empire of China in 221 B.C. His conquests united the many states that had fought each other for years in China. He called himself "August Sovereign," the name that all emperors of China used afterward. He was the founder of the Qin dynasty. Dynasties are periods of rule by members of the same family, and most of China's long history is divided into dynasties, beginning in about 1994 B.C. with the Xia dynasty and lasting until A.D. 1911, with the end of the Qing dynasty. The political system of the three earliest dynasties, the Xia, Shang, and Zhou, was a feudal system. The dynasties that followed, beginning with the Qin, were centralized empires.

Chapter 2

HISTORY

China is the birthplace of the world's oldest continuous civilization, with a written history that began 3,500 years ago. Humans have lived in what is now China long before history was recorded Archaeological evidence shows that humans who made tools were living in China at least twelve thousand years ago. They lived in dwellings dug into the earth and roofed over. Pigs and dogs had been domesticated and pottery making had been learned.

The Xia, Shang, and Zhou Dynasties

By 2205 B.C., China consisted of a number of small states that, according to tradition, were conquered and united by the Xia dynasty (1994 to 1523 B.C.). From that dynasty until A.D. 1911, the history of China tells of the rise and fall of dynasties. The first historical dynasty, the Shang dynasty, dates from 1523 to 1027 B.C.

The Shang kings were powerful rulers, with great armies at their command. They could send from three thousand to five thousand soldiers into battle at a time. The soldiers in these armies used bronze weapons that included a complex bow and arrow and a halberd. The army was driven to the scene of battle by chariots and would then dismount to begin fighting.

The Shang dynasty was overthrown by the Zhou dynasty, whose rule lasted from 1027 to 221 B.C. Under the Zhou dynasty, the government extended its control into north and south China by conquest and planned settlements. In the later period of Zhou rule, the central government's control became less strong. This period, known as the Spring and Autumn period, saw the growth of independent states. These states paid only a small allegiance to the central government.

An array of reproduced weapons on the
Great Wall of China. Soldiers in the armies
of the Shang kings used bronze weapons.

The Warring States Period

By 475 B.C., the independent states began fighting each other so often that the period from 475 to 221 has come to be called the Warring States period. Its end also marked the end of the Zhou dynasty.[1] Warfare was waged with the composite bow, whose arrows were made with bronze or clay points. Other weapons used during this period of warfare included bronze spears, battle-axes, and halberds.

The End of War: The Qin Dynasty

In 221 B.C., peace was restored to the empire when China became united under the Qin dynasty and the First Emperor, Shi Huangdi. During the Qin dynasty, the language, writing and currency of China was standardized, and the vast empire was united by a vast system of roads and canals.

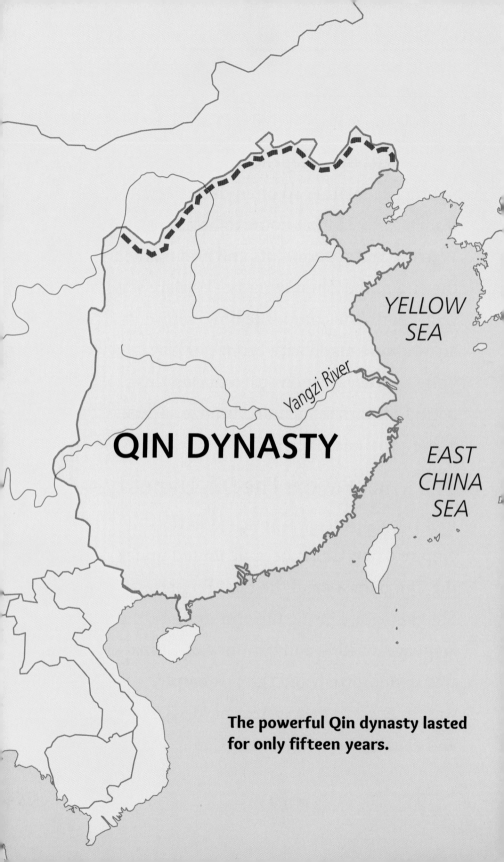

YELLOW
SEA

Yangzi River

QIN DYNASTY

EAST
CHINA
SEA

**The powerful Qin dynasty lasted
for only fifteen years.**

Despite its lasting influence, the Qin dynasty ruled for only fifteen years. This dynasty ended with the murder of the First Emperor's son in 207 B.C. Rebellion and civil war had broken out even before that event, however. From these warring groups emerged a farmer who lost every battle but his last one. Liu Pang, also known as Han Gaozu, the first commoner to rule China, became the first emperor to rule over the Han dynasty.[2]

The Han Dynasty

The Han dynasty continued the rule of China under a powerful central government. The empire was divided into fourteen commanderies and ten kingdoms ruled by the emperor's sons or nobles he appointed. The powerful bureaucracy that had been set up by the Qin dynasty was expanded to reinforce the control of the central government.

**A gourd-shaped drinking vessel
from the Zhou dynasty.**

It was during this period that government inspectors were sent to all regions of the empire. They reported back to the central office in the capital on the conditions and the administration in each of the inspector's districts. The inspectors communicated with the capital via a postal system, which was set up along the main highways that linked the empire.

The money to run the government came from taxes. A land tax and a head tax were imposed on the people. State income also came from taxes paid on silk and revenues that came from government-owned industries such as salt and iron.

The Han dynasty continued its rule from 206 B.C. until A.D. 220, except for a fifteen-year period from A.D. 8 to A.D. 23. During those years, Wang Mang's Xin dynasty ruled China. But the Xin dynasty did not last for long. After which the Han dynasty was successfully restored.

**A jade water container created
during the Han Dynasty**

....

Because of the interruption caused by
Wang Mang, the Han dynasty was divided
into the Former Han, or Western Han
(206 B.C. to A.D. 8), and the Later Han, or
Eastern Han (A.D. 23 to 220).

The Han dynasty had vast armies at its
command and was able to expand the
empire a great deal. In 137 B.C., the Han
emperor sent an army of three hundred

thousand men to Mongolia. Within ten years, the Han controlled Inner Mongolia. The Han then took control of Korea between 109 and 106 B.C. By 82 B.C. the Han dynasty had extended China's borders to Burma.

The armies of the Han dynasty were made up of farmers and professional soldiers as well as mercenary troops who were recruited from north of the empire's borders. At the age of thirty, every man in the empire had to enroll and serve one year in the army. For those men who served on the frontiers of the empire, service was permanent.

However, as powerful as the Han armies were, they were never able to conquer the nomad tribes north of China, beyond what became known as the Great Wall. That wall was begun by the First Emperor and was expanded under later dynasties to keep out invading nomads

According to Chinese legend, the Great Wall is really a huge dragon turned to stone. The length of the wall was broken at intervals by watchtowers. It originally stretched for 3,700 miles along China's border.

from China's north. But It failed to do so. Invasion and attack from north of the wall was a frequent threat in ancient China until northern tribes finally succeeded in conquering China.

Dynasties rose and fell in the centuries after the Han dynasty and China's conquest by the Mongols and the Qing dynasty. But the powerful central state created by the Qin dynasty, which had been expanded and strengthened by the Han dynasty, remained in place until the end of the empire in A.D. 1911. The concept of a powerful and virtuous emperor ruling through a vast bureaucracy under strict law and strongly influenced by philosophies of the time was adapted and used by the succeeding dynasties.

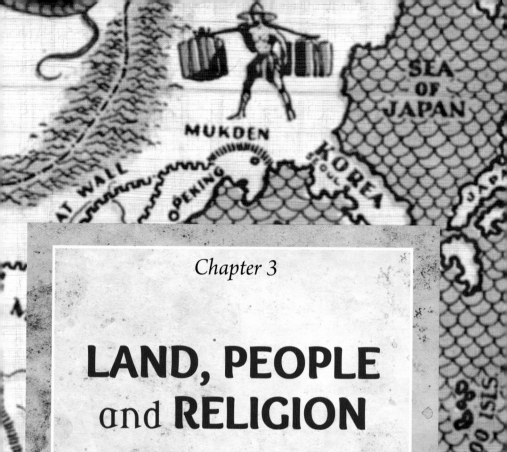

Chapter 3

LAND, PEOPLE and RELIGION

China is the largest country in the world in population and the fourth-largest in area. China's east coast is bordered by three seas, the Yellow Sea, the East China Sea, and the South China Sea, which are all part of the Pacific Ocean. China's northern border reaches Mongolia and Russia while to the south, China reaches North Vietnam. To the west, China's major neighbor is India.

Northern China was and is cold and dry, suitable only for the cultivation of wheat or barley and millet and pasture for some horses and cattle. Most important to the people in northern China is the deposit by wind and dust storms of a rich, fertile soil known as loess. Loess deposits, which can be hundreds of feet deep, provided shelter for the ancient Chinese, since they were able to dig homes in them. Southern China was warm and tropical in part and suitable for the cultivation of rice, tea, and mulberry trees whose leaves provided the food for silkworms. Those silkworms provided the Chinese with the material to make silk, which was also produced in other regions. Silk has been an important material throughout Chinese history.

Major Rivers

The two major rivers in China are the Yellow River (Huang He) and the Yangzi River (Chang Jiang). The Yellow River runs for approximately 3,395 miles, from the Kunlun Mountains in western China to the Bo Hai, an arm of the Yellow Sea, in the east, but its course has changed—or been changed—over the centuries. The Yellow River has overflowed its banks countless times in China's long history, causing flooding over thousands of miles. That flooding has led to a vast deposit of loess from which the early centers of China grew.[1]

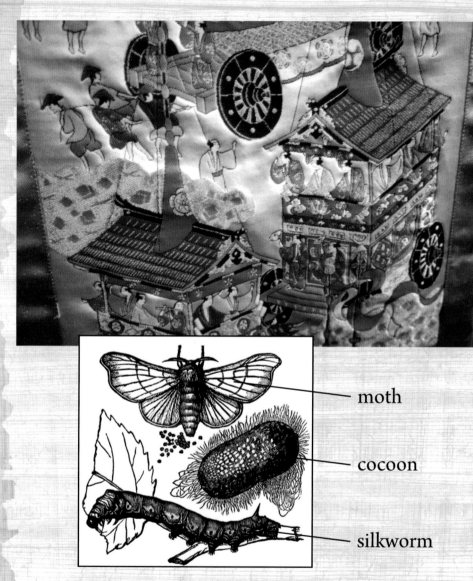

moth

cocoon

silkworm

According to a Chinese legend, silk was discovered in about 2700 B.C. in Emperor Haungdi's garden. Only the Chinese knew how to make silk for 3,000 years.

China's longest river is the Yangzi, flowing 3,200 miles from the Tibetan plateau to the East China Sea. The Yangzi is the longest river in Asia and the third longest river in the world. Unlike the Yellow River, the Yangzi is navigable. Large ships can navigate the Yangzi for up to 1,000 miles from the coast to the interior of China, after which smaller ships can travel an additional 600 miles.[2] Throughout China's history, the Yangzi has been a highway of communication, commerce, and trade from China's coast deep into its interior. China is roughly divided into north and south regions by a line drawn midway between the Yellow River and the Yangzi River.

Farming and Mining

Agriculture was the main occupation of the Chinese under the Shang kings and through the Han Empire. There were few

The Yangzi River has always played a major role in Chinese history. For thousands of years, people have used the river for water, irrigation, sanitation, transportation, industry, boundary-marking and war.

cities except those established as capitals
by the kings and emperors or local centers
for the administration of the government.
Most of the population lived in small towns
and villages whose inhabitants were connected by family or clan ties.

While the majority of the population
was made up of farmers, there were significant numbers of skilled artisans such as
bronze makers, potters, and even makers of
musical instruments such as bells and
ocarinas, which are oval wind instruments.[3]
Beginning in the Qin dynasty and greatly
expanded under the Han dynasty, there
was a large bureaucracy of government
officials.

Farmers paid rent to the government in
the form of crops or labor to live on the
land they farmed. They were also forced to
donate some of their time to work on
dikes, roads, and public buildings. Forced
labor was also used to build defensive walls

of rammed earth with the hardness of cement around the cities and larger towns. There were small numbers of merchants who lived in the capital cities or traveled the countryside.

By the Shang dynasty, 1523 B.C. to 1027 B.C., bronze was in wide use, and the Shang kings used chariots and weapons of bronze. Iron, first cast in 513 B.C., was in general use by 400 B.C., mainly in agriculture. With the invention of the bellows, steel was being produced in China by the second century B.C.

Early Writing

The history of Shang rule is derived from vast numbers of bones and tortoise shells discovered in Anyang, one of the Shang kings' capitals. The bones and shells are inscribed with questions asked by the kings and answers given by specialists practiced in the art of interpreting the cracks and

A view of the Yellow River in China's Sichuan Province where it winds through the Tangke Grassland.

markings in the bones and shells that were produced by heating them. This practice was known as divination. Oracles, people who were considered to have a special wisdom and the ability to foretell the future, would read the cracks in the bones and answer questions asked of them by government officials. Those questions might be about almost anything, because it is believed that the Shang kings were highly superstitious. But they probably asked questions about the worship of ancestors, what military actions should be taken, and whether those actions would be successful.

In addition to the bones and tortoise shells, official accounts are also derived from writings on bamboo and wood. The existence of these written records shows that writing was already highly developed by the Shang period. Its origin in China is still unknown.[4]

Religion

Religion in China by the time of the Shang dynasty was made up of many elements. Ancestor worship was one of the many features of early Chinese religion. Ancestor worship was limited to the wealthier classes until the Han dynasty. Farmers and their families devoted their worship mainly to local gods asking for good crops and family health. The various gods were honored with ceremonies, and sacrifices were carried out by heads of families. One of the rituals was divination, which often was performed to determine whether ancestors desired specific sacrifices or rituals. As society became more organized, state officials, including the king, performed certain rites and ceremonies.

There was no official class of priests in ancient China.[5] But worship was conducted with help from an individual known

According to legend, the use of tea was discovered by Emperor Shennong of China about 2737 B.C. The earliest known mention of tea appeared in Chinese literature of about A.D. 350. These workers are planting tea in present-day China.

as a shaman. Shamans enlisted the help of certain animals who were thought to have a special connection with the ancestors whose advice and assistance were being sought.[6] Kings and emperors also assumed the role of shaman.

In the Shang dynasty, religion differed from place to place, each area having its own local god. Many gods were the same gods with different names. Ultimately the government made one god, Shangdi, the Lord on High, the official god. Kings and ministers were worshiped after their deaths because it was believed that they could approach Shangdi, the supreme god, on behalf of the common people.

In 1027 B.C., the Zhou dynasty conquered the Shang dynasty. Under the Zhou human sacrifice was officially forbidden.[7] Until then, humans as well as animals including cattle, dogs, and pigs were sacrificed to the gods. Most of the humans sacrificed were prisoners of war. But villagers may have fought and captured people from other villages for human sacrifice.[8] Human sacrifice was also made during burial ceremonies of kings. The thousands of terra-cotta soldiers buried near the First Emperor's tomb may have been a substitute for the burial of actual soldiers. The First Emperor had the massive warrior army constructed in order to accompany him into the afterlife and protect him there

A significant part of ancient Chinese religion was based on certain philosophies that were more concerned with human relationships than with a person's relationship to a personal god. The philosophies addressed the question of how to organize society and a person's relationship with others for his or her own good and the greater good of the state.

Philosophies: Legalism, Confucianism, and Taoism

Ancient China was home to three schools of philosophy that have affected thought and behavior throughout its history. These schools of philosophy are known as Legalism, Confucianism, and Taoism.

Legalism

Legalism is the belief that society must be built on law and serve the interest of the state. Legalism continued to exert a strong influence up to modern times and was particularly powerful in its effect on the governments of the Qin and Han dynasties.

As Legalism was practiced, judges were supposed to correctly identify a crime and its punishment as specifically set forth in law. Strict law must define the crime and its punishment and not be subject to interpretation by the judge or other individuals.[9]

Underlying Legalism is the belief in a powerful centralized state run by officials who are appointed by a ruler who must be obeyed without question. The law, which could not be questioned, had to be made known to the public and administered according to specific rules and regulations.

By the time of the Han dynasty, the law was to be applied equally to all, commoners as well as the those in the nobility. But by the late Han dynasty, there were distinctions based on rank in how the law was applied.

Confucianism

According to Chinese tradition, Confucius was a thinker, political figure, educator. Confucius (551–479 B.C.), whose teachings led to a school of philosophy, lived during the second half of the Zhou dynasty (1027–221 B.C.). His teachings have had a profound effect on China throughout its history. Confucianism became the official philosophy in the Han dynasty. It dominated Chinese thought to the end of the empire in 1911.

Little is known about Confucius's life. Modern scholars base most of what they do know on a collection of his sayings and stories about his life collected by his followers that were written down after Confucius's death. This collection, called the *Analects*, was added to over the centuries by other writers of philosophy.

Confucius taught that man's relationships with others begins in the family, from father to son, elder brother to younger brother. Good relationships within the family, beginning with those between father and son, extend to one's relationship to strangers and finally to the relationship between the ruler and his subjects. He did not teach about a personal god or even promote a doctrine of religion. He did include in his teachings the doctrine of the

Mandate of Heaven and the belief in Destiny. The Mandate of Heaven states that Heaven calls for the most virtuous man to be China's ruler. If that man loses his virtue, he will in turn lose the Mandate of Heaven, and his dynasty will be overthrown. Destiny, beyond human control, dictated one's condition in life by determining a person's wealth and health.[10]

Belief in the Mandate of Heaven and Destiny was central to Confucius's teaching because it meant that people should behave in a way that fit in with their position in life. Confucius did not believe that humans should lead passive lives, however. Instead, he urged people to devote themselves to living a moral life that followed the Way of Heaven as taught by the ancient sages.[11]

According to Confucius, every man had the potential and duty to reach the same state of virtue, or level of goodness, that the ancient sages had achieved. While

Confucius (center) is depicted on a visit to the Court of Ch'u. No book definitely written by Confucius exists. His disciples recorded his conversations and sayings in a book called the *Analects*.

acknowledging that Destiny was in control of the human condition, he believed that humans had the free will to choose to live good lives.

In Confucian thought, virtue could only be achieved within a carefully ordered society, which could only come about when selfishness and greed were overcome by all people within that society. The way to virtue was by achieving benevolence, which happened when people considered others before themselves.[12] In order to know virtue, it was the duty of every man to study the ancient sages, considered the source of all virtue. People were able to gain knowledge about these sages by studying books, especially those known as the *Wu Jing* (Wu Ching), or Five Classics.

One of those books, called the *Book of Changes*, includes ancient Chinese beliefs about the universe. Another book that is entitled the *Book of Rituals* describes the rules governing all behavior between people. It also describes rites and rituals, including religious ceremonies such as those honoring ancestors.[13]

Mencius (or Mengzi), who lived from 371 to 289 B.C., expanded upon the teachings of Confucius. Mencius taught that humans are basically good, but that goodness must be strengthened by practicing rites and rituals. That practice allowed one's goodness to overcome the constant threat of selfishness, considered part of human nature.

Taoism

A philosopher who lived at the same time as Confucius was the father of a very different school of thought. His teachings were followed by many during the Han dynasty even though Confucianism was the official philosophy. This philosopher is known as Lao Zi (Lao Tzu). Lao Tzi was born in the sixth century B.C. and he was acquainted with Confucius. His philosophy, known as Taoism, is contained in the *Lao Zi* (*Lao Tzu*), or *Daodejing* (*Tao Te Ching*). The *Lao Zi*, which translates as "Classic of the Way and Virtue," is written in parables and verse. It calls for humans to live in natural harmony with the Tao, or Dao, which is considered a cosmic unity that underlies all things. Taoism, unlike Confucianism, teaches that the best government is the one that governs the least.[14] The less people strive, and the less the government interferes, the happier all will be. Taoism is based on one's acceptance of his or her natural state. In Taoism, striving to move ahead in society is considered harmful.

Taoism also opposed the practice of the rites and ceremonies that were practiced by the followers of Confucius's teachings. According to tradition, in a meeting between Confucius and Lao Zi,

Lao Tzi is depicted in this sixth century image. He was the founder of Taoism. He wrote a book that explained his beliefs called the *Tao Te Ching*.

Lao Zi implied that the rites were only the words of dead men and therefore useless.[15]

Like Confucianism, Taoism sought order in one's personal life as well as in the state. But unlike Confucianism, Taoism taught that the ruler must avoid actions such as honoring individuals or creating items that could lead to desire. A passage from the *Daodejing* makes this quite plain.

> There is no crime greater than having too many desires; There is no disaster greater than not being content; There is no misfortune greater than being covetous.[16]

China was, and is, a land of many different cultures. One reason why Chinese civilization has endured can be traced to the beliefs of its people and the teachings of its philosophers.

Chapter 4

Family Life:
EDUCATION, FOOD, CLOTHING, SHELTER

In ancient China, most families lived on farms. The ancient Chinese farm was generally small, only about fifteen acres. All the members of a family worked on a farm. Under the Zhou Dynasty, certain sections of a farmer's land were set aside for the nobility. The noble's land was worked by serfs, who were bound under the feudal system to work on a farm but did not own the land. They were subject to the will of the landowner. Farming was hard work, as farmers' tools at the time were mostly made of bone, wood, and stone. With the unification of China under the Qin dynasty, however, feudalism was abolished, people could own land, and individuals were taxed by the government.

The Development of the Calendar

It was essential for a farmer to know when to begin planting his crops. One of the most important functions of the emperor was to inform farmers of the proper time to begin planting. During the Shang dynasty, the development of a calendar was already under way. In it, a week consisted of ten days, and each day was measured by ten "Heavenly Stems" and twelve "Earthly Branches" in a recurring cycle of sixty days.

By 104 B.C., during the Han dynasty, the four seasons as we now know them were first fixed according to a calendar based on the spring and fall equinoxes and summer and winter solstices. Under Emperor Wang Mang, who ruled from A.D. 8 to 23 after overthrowing the Han dynasty, the year was calculated to consist of just over 365 days.

Clay, Cloth, and Other Early Materials

The ancient Chinese were skilled in the firing of clay to produce a hard pottery. Metal was too scarce and valuable at the time to be used except for coins and weapons. Pottery was a useful substitute for metal, particularly for storing things.

Plant fibers such as hemp were used to make cloth. Wool came into use under the Zhou dynasty. Silk was already an important product under the Shang dynasty. Silk was expensive and only used for robes worn in official ceremonies. Silk became the chief export under the Han dynasty, both as gifts to foreign rulers and in trade. Silk in the Han dynasty was exported throughout central Asia, to northern India, and farther west throughout the Roman Empire.[1] The trade route used to transport silk became known as the Silk Road.

The Ancient Chinese Home

In the capital city, houses were made of stone and mud bricks. The homes of the weathy were built of wood with roofs supported by pillars resting on stone or bronze bases. Many of these homes, except for those of wealthy people, were a place of both family life and work.

In some areas of the countryside, homes were carved out of the sides of mountains or dug deep into the thick compact loess, deposits of silt or clay, for insulation against the cold in the winter and the heat of the summer. Rectangular or oval homes had roofs that were thatched with reeds or straw, with their lower levels set deep in the ground. Housing above the ground appears to have become common-place around the period of the Warring States, from 475 to 221 B.C., which pre-ceded the Qin dynasty.[2]

Food in Ancient China

Food preparation as an art began in China more than three thousand years ago. The foods eaten and prepared by the people of ancient China were as varied as the regions themselves. Chinese cuisine

Chinese houses had curved roofs created to keep away evil spirits. Spirits were believed to travel in straight lines and it was thought that curved roofs would confuse them.

was, and remains, an important part of
Chinese culture, and in ancient times,
cooking was considered an activity that
distinguished civilizations. That food and
cooking were important to the ancient
Chinese can be seen in a legend about Tang,
an emperor of the Shang dynasty, who
chose a famous chef, Yi Yen, to be his prime
minister. Records also show that more than
two thousand people who were on the staff
of the imperial palace during the Western
Zhou dynasty were kept busy preparing
food for the emperor and his wife.[3]

Chinese cuisine is believed to have
originated in the Shang period, and it is
during this time that historians believe the
Chinese mastered the techniques of steam-
ing, stir-frying, and deep-frying that are still
used to prepare Chinese food. Rice and
wheat were staples, but a balanced diet,
considered important for both physical and
spiritual well-being, contained vegetables

Rice, along with wheat, were staples. Vegetables, like bean sprouts, were considered important for both physical and spiritual well-being.

and fruits as well as meat and fish. The upper classes were able to enjoy a wide variety of meat, including horse, cow, chicken, pig, sheep, and deer, while fish was often the best that commoners could get. Yet everyone feasted on some important holidays. There were also feast for weddings and other major events. Special dishes were served at these banquets.

However, the banquets of the rich were the most special. At these there were many different foods to choose from. Besides the a variety of different kinds of vegetables, roasted duck, pheasant, and wild boar, might be served. Sometimes an unusual dish such as bear's paws was brought out.

Recent archaeological findings of ancient bronze wares have shed light on what the ancient Chinese ate, since these vessels have been found with food remains. They also show how the ancient Chinese prepared their food. The ding was the most important bronze vessel used to cook meat. It could be either round, with three legs, or rectangular, with four legs, and was elevated to allow a fire underneath. Rice was usually cooked in a li, which had hollow, pouchlike legs that held water. The other main kind of cooking vessel was the yan, which was used to steam foods. It had pouchlike legs like a li and an upper part like the top of a ding, but a rack was connected to its base so that the food could be cooked by steam. The Chinese practice of cutting foods into bite-size pieces during preparation, rather than at the dinner table, began during this period and has continued to this day.

Education for the Wealthy

In ancient China, many farmers taught their sons farming, mothers taught their daughters household skills, and artisans taught their children and their apprentices their crafts, but roles within families were

Large-scale terrace farming is used in mountainous and hilly regions of China.

not always so tied to gender. But formal education was limited to those in wealthy families who could afford tutors. It was not until the age of Confucius, 551 B.C. to 479 B.C., that mass education began in ancient China. By 165 B.C., written examinations were being given to select government officials.[4] In 124 B.C., an imperial academy was created for the study of Confucian texts. Fifty students attended the academy. This system of government-sponsored academies was greatly expanded later under the Han dynasty.

In these academies, students memorized the texts of books that were written on wooden tablets, thin sheets of bamboo, or lengths of silk. These books were texts on medicine and warfare and collections of poetry and philosophy. Students were not permitted to give their own interpretation of the texts.[5] There were no gym classes or recess. Students would study from early morning to late afternoon. Discipline was strict and included beatings. The schools were mainly for the education of government workers and reflected the thinking that the government wanted to promote. Successful students were then enrolled in government service.

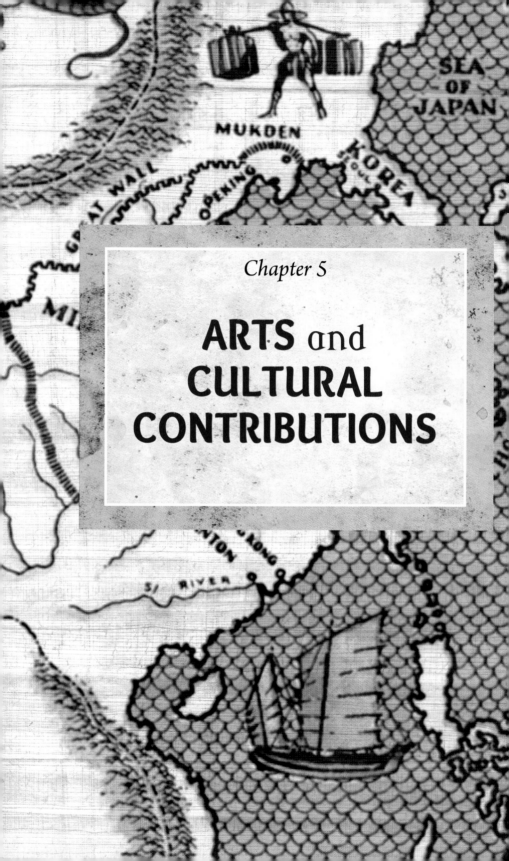

Chapter 5

ARTS and CULTURAL CONTRIBUTIONS

The oldest Chinese art that has survived from thousands of years ago is in the form of pottery and bronze. By the time of the Shang dynasty, brilliant white earthenware vessels were being fired, or made in kilns or ovens. They were decorated by patterns painted onto the surface of the vessel. China's achievement in the art of pottery is considered among the finest in human history.

Bronzes, Pottery, and Paintings

During the Shang dynasty, bronze vessels, statues, and even bells were made and are considered among the finest bells ever produced. The bronze vessels were mainly used for religious ceremonies. They were decorated with pictures of birds and other animals, particularly water buffalo sporting tiger's teeth. In the Han dynasty, bronzes were inlaid with precious metals, such as gold and silver, depicting scenes from history, ritual ceremonies, and legends.

Pottery continued to be the main material from which everyday items were made. In the later Han dynasty, glazed pottery and porcelain began to be used. Clay was used to make models of people, animals, and houses. Ancient Chinese potters also made beautiful vases, some from procelain.

Painting, mostly on silk, was highly developed, and the subjects included humans and landscapes. Tomb paintings from the Han dynasty show scenes depicting human figures and landscapes.

Painting was another valued art in ancient China. Many of the painters did landscapes. These frequently featured mountains and water. The artists tried to capture the peace, harmony, and beauty of nature in their work.

Pottery recovered from an ancient tomb of the Western Han dynasty.

This Shang dynasty bronze in the shape of a bird is called a Xiaoyou (a kind of drinking vessel).

A piece of pottery dating back to the Qin dynasty.

This landscape painting on silk was created between 1279 and 960 B.C.

A museum official at the Hong Kong Museum of Art looks at a pale yellowish-green jade Chimera with a rider of the late Eastern Han dynasty.

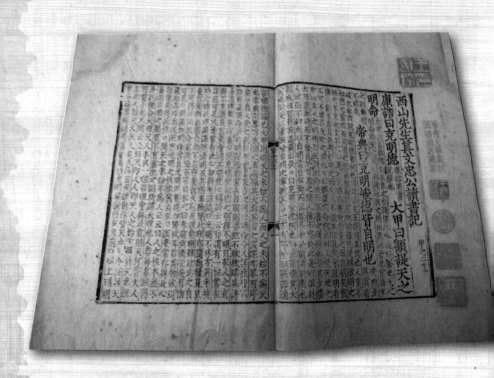

Perhaps the greatest Chinese invention was paper and with it, printing.

Before the Chinese invented paper money (much like we use today), they mostly used coins.

··

The First Paper

Ancient China's greatest contribution to world culture from the period may well be that of paper. It was first manufactured and used in ancient China in the first century A.D. and began to be widely used in China by the third or fourth century A.D.[1]

Woodblock printing was commonly done on paper by the seventh century A.D. 868. By the ninth century, the Chinese had come up with both paper playing cards and paper money. Between A.D. 1041 and 1048, the Chinese invented a movable type press. This invention would help to make books and other printed materials available worldwide. It was not until twelve hundred years later that paper was first manufactured in Italy. Its discovery spread from China to Syria, Iraq, and Egypt before making its way to Italy.

Chapter 6

GOVERNMENT

The first ruler of the Shang dynasty united a number of small kingdoms in 1523 B.C. after years of war. The Shang dynasty was led by a king who ruled through aristocratic families appointed to govern throughout the kingdom. The king was the leader of the armies and also acted as a priest. He was succeeded in rule by his sons or his brothers. The Shang kings waged aggressive wars and expanded their rule by founding new towns as farmers' settlements. Records of government activities from this period come from inscriptions on the divination bones and shells that have been excavated by archaeologists, particularly from one of the Shang capitals at Anyang.

The Zhou Dynasty

Under the Zhou dynasty, which overthrew the Shang dynasty in 1027 B.C., kings continued to rule the government, and they were succeeded by their sons. The king, assisted by relatives and aristocratic families, ruled over a population of about 13.7 million. Various regions of the Zhou kingdom were given to individuals to govern. Those people then pledged their military support and allegiance to the Zhou king.

The appointment of local rulers led to a growing independence of various regions, and the central government's authority

This drawing offers one representation of the "First Emperor" of China, the Qin emperor Shi Huangdi.

grew less powerful. In the period 771 to 476 B.C., known as the Spring and Autumn period, these regions had grown to be semi-independent states whose loyalty to the Zhou king was waning.[1]

From 475 B.C. to 221 B.C., although the Zhou kings remained in power, these regions constantly warred with each other. This period in Chinese history is known as the Warring States period.

The Qin Dynasty Unites the Empire

The chaos and constant warfare of the Warring States period ended in 221 B.C., when the rulers of the Zhou dynasty as well as the various states were conquered and overthrown by the Qin dynasty. It was with the Qin dynasty that China's centralized form of government began. The Qin dynasty was founded by Shi Huangdi who was known as the First Emperor. He was assisted by a minister, Li Si, who followed the theories of Legalism to build a strong centralized state under the emperor's rule.

However, while the Legalism principles had the greatest influence under the First Emperor, Confucianism and Taoism still existed. The First Emperor was interested in Taoism's mystical elements, especially that certain magic potions might give him eternal life. [2]

The First Emperor and Li Si set about unifying the new empire. They divided it into thirty-six regions called command-eries. Each region was governed by officials appointed by the central government based in the empire's capital. This governing system was expanded in the Han dynasty. There, three senior officials were put in charge of nine ministers, each heading a different ministry. These senior officials

The Shang kings expanded their rule by founding new towns as farmers' settlements. Shown here is a modern-day farming village in China.

Coins were introduced during the Qin dynasty. The coins were round with holes in the center.

were assisted by large staffs of assistants, clerks, and advisors.[3]

Standardized Writing and Coins

One most important change made by the First Emperor was the standardization of the written language. At the time of the First Emperor's conquest, written Chinese consisted of many different languages and dialects. The dialects were so different from each other that people in one region often could not understand the writings of people from another region. By developing a standard form of writing, the ruler of the Qin dynasty ensured that the written word would have the same meaning throughout the vast reaches of his empire, although the spoken dialects of China have remained varied throughout its history. Weights and measurements as well as coins were also standardized in this period.

The government also melted down all weapons not used for warfare, and the metal was used to make statues and memorials to the First Emperor. The ancient walls around selected cities and towns that had separated them were torn down. Roads and canals were built, further unifying the empire. Even the width of the axles of the carts that traveled these new roads was fixed by the government.

According to Chinese legend, the Great Wall is really a huge dragon turned to stone. It was built to protect China's northern border from invading tribes.

....

The Great Wall Begins

In the north, the many defensive walls built as early as 300 B.C. began to be connected. This project was the beginning of what would much later become the Great Wall of China. It was built to keep out northern invaders and mark the northern border of the empire.

Pain and Progress

Despite all his accomplishments, the First
Emperor was also known for the harsh
treatment meted out to his people. To
further unify the empire and crush all his
opponents, he destroyed thousands of
historical records and books, except for
scientific texts and certain religious texts.
No one was allowed to oppose his will.
One hundred and twenty thousand of the
leading families in the empire were forced
to move to the capital. In one brutal act, he
ordered 460 opponents of his regime to be
executed by burning or burying them alive.

The basic form of government that was
established by the First Emperor and Li Si
existed until the revolution of 1911, when
China became a republic. But the First
Emperor's dynasty was ended by popular
rebellion in the third year of the reign of
his youngest son, who succeeded him.

The Grand Canal in China begins at Beijing and ends at Hangzhou. It is the longest canal in China as well as in the world.

The Han Dynasty

In the year 207 B.C., a new dynasty began
to rule China called the Han Dynasty. It
would rule China for the next 400 years.
During this time period they would be one
of the wealthiest and most powerful
nations on Earth. The Han dynasty, which
followed the Qin dynasty, was influenced
by the doctrine of Legalism. Its rulers kept
and expanded the strong central government that had begun under Shi Huangdi's
rule. The Han emperors also favored
Taoism, but they adopted Confucianism as
the official state philosophy. Unlike the
First Emperor, Shi Huangdi, the emperors
of the Han dynasty allowed other philosophies and ideas, especially Taoism, to be
practiced.[4]

Through conquest and natural growth,
China's population under the Han dynasty
soared. In the year 2 B.C., as the Western

Han dynasty was approaching its end, the government census showed that the population of the empire was 59.6 million in 12.2 million households.

The Hans were contemporaries of the Romans. Their empire was just as powerful, included as many people and was almost as large as the Roman empire. The world population was around 180 million in A.D. 100. Four-fifths of the world's population at that time lived under the Chinese Han, Roman, and Indian Gupta empires.

TIMELINE

Xia c.1994–c. 1523 B.C.

Agriculture developed; bronze used

Shang c. 1523–1027 B.C.

First calendar; uniform writing

Zhou 1027–221 B.C. Age of Confucius; use of money and iron; first written laws

   Spring and Autumn Period 771–476 B.C.
   Growth of independent states
   Warring States Period 475–221 B.C.
   Warfare with bows, spears, halberds

Qin 221–207 B.C.

China unified; Great Wall begun; roads built; written Chinese standardized

Han 206 B.C.

Central rule strengthened; Buddhism introduced; postal system; taxes imposed

   Western Han 206 b.c.–A.D.
   Wang Mang A.D. 8–23
   Eastern Han A.D. 23–220

GLOSSARY

ancestor—A person from who a family or group descends.

A.D.—An abbreviation for the Latin anno Domini, meaning "in the year of our Lord." Used for a measurement of time, A.D. indicates the number of years since the supposed birth date of Christ.

archaeology—A study of the remains of early people.

artisan—A skilled craftsperson.

B.C.—Before Christ. Used for a measurement of time, B.C. indicates the number of years before the supposed birth date of Christ.

chariot—A two-wheeled carriage pulled by horses.

chimera—An imaginary monster compounded of many incongruous parts.

civilization—An organized society that has developed social customs, government, technology, and the arts.

Glossary

culture—A people's way of life.

dialect— A form of spoken in a certain district or by a certain group of people.

dynasty—A series of rulers who belong to the same family.

emperor—The head of an empire.

empire—A nation and the country it rules.

equinox—Either of the two times of the year when day and night are of equal length everywhere on earth.

loess—A fertile yellow topsoil believed to be chiefly deposited by the wind.

nomad—A person who wanders from place to place.

philosophy—A way of thinking.

terra-cotta—A glazed or unglazed fired clay used especially for statuettes and vases and architectural purposes.

CHAPTER NOTES

Chapter 1. AN ARMY PROTECTS THE FIRST EMPEROR

1. Jane O'Connor, *The Emperor's Silent Army* (New York: Penguin Group, 2002), p. 30.
2. J.A.G. Roberts, *A Concise History of China* (Cambridge, Mass.: Harvard University Press, 1999), p. 25.

Chapter 2. HISTORY

1. Dun J. Li, *The Ageless Chinese: A History* (New York: Charles Scribner's Sons, 1965), p. 45.
2. Ibid., pp. 103–104.

Chapter 3. LAND, PEOPLE, AND RELIGION

1. W. Scott Morton, *China: Its History and Culture* (New York: Lippincott & Crowell, 1980), p. 6.
2. Dun J. Li, *The Ageless Chinese:* A History (New York: Charles Scribner's Sons, 1965), p. 8.
3. L. Carrington Goodrich, A *Short History of the Chinese People* (New York: Harper & Row, 1963), p. 17.
4. Morton, p. 18.
5. Ibid., p. 31.

6. John King Fairbank, *China: A New History* (Cambridge, Mass.: The Belknap Press of Harvard University Press, 1992), p. 37.
7. Wolfram Eberhard, *A History of China* (Berkeley and Los Angeles: University of California Press, 1969), p. 22.
8. Ibid., p. 23.
9. Jacques Gernet, *A History of Chinese Civilization* (New York: Cambridge University Press, 1982), p. 91.
10. Leslie Stevenson and David L. Haberman, *Ten Theories of Human Nature* (New York: The Oxford University Press, 1998), pp. 26–27.
11. Ibid., p. 27.
12. Ibid., p. 35.
13. Ibid., p. 36.
14. Li, p. 85.
15. Lao Tzu, *Tao Te Ching: Translated with an introduction by D. C. Lau* (London, Great Britain: Penguin Books, 1963), p. viii.
16. Ibid., p. xxv.

Chapter 4. FAMILY LIFE: EDUCATION, FOOD, CLOTHING, SHELTER

1. Jacques Gernet, *A History of Chinese Civilization* (New York: Cambridge University Press, 1982), p. 133.
2. Michael Loewe and Edward L. Shaughnessy, *The Cambridge History of Ancient China From the Origins of Civilization to 221 B.C.* (New York: Cambridge University Press, 1999), p. 455.

3. "3,000-Year-Old Food for Thought," China Daily, March 13, 2003, <http://www.china.org.cn/english/culture/58121.htm> (November 20, 2003).
4. L. Carrington Goodrich, *A Short History of the Chinese People* (New York: Harper & Row, 1963), p. 51.
5. Kenneth Scott Latourette, *The Chinese: Their History and Culture* (New York: Macmillan, 1962), p. 661.

Chapter 5. ARTS AND CULTURAL CONTRIBUTIONS

1. Michael Loewe and Edward L. Shaughnessy, *The Cambridge History of Ancient China From the Origins of Civilization to 221B.C.* (New York: Cambridge University Press, 1999), p. 650.

Chapter 6. GOVERNMENT

1. L. Carrington Goodrich, *A Short History of the Chinese People* (New York: Harper & Row, 1963), pp. 19–21.
2. Michael Loewe & Edward L. Shaughnessy, *The Cambridge History of Ancient China From the Origins of Civilization to 221 B.C.* (New York: Cambridge University Press, 1999), p. 78.
3. Ibid., p. 1,017.
4. Dun J. Li, *The Ageless Chinese: A History* (New York: Charles Scribner's Sons, 1965), p. 115.

FURTHER READING

BOOKS

Allan, Tony. *Ancient China*. New York: Chelsea House Publishers: 2007.

Anderson, Dale. *Ancient China*. Chicago, Illinois: Raintree, 2005.

Ball, Jacqueline and Richard Levey. *Ancient China: Archaeology Unlocks the Secrets of China's Past.* Washington, D.C: National Geographic, 2007.

Binns, Tristan Boyer. *Ancient Chinese*. Minneapolis, Minn.: Compass Point Books, 2007.

Challen, Paul. *Life in Ancient China*. St. Catharines, Ont.: Crabtree Pub., 2005.

Deady, Kathleen and Muriel L. Dubois. *Ancient China: Beyond the Great Wall*. Mankato, Minn.: Capstone Press, 2012.

Portal, Jane. *Terra Cotta Warriors: Guardians of China's First Emperor*. Washington, D.C.: National Geographic, 2008.

Shuter, Jane. *Ancient China*. Chicago, Illinois: Raintree, 2007.

INTERNET ADDRESSES

Ancient Chinese Life.com: Ancient Chinese Facts for Kids
<http://www.ancientchinalife.com/ ancient-china-children.html>

National Geographic Kids: Facts and Photos: China
<http://kids.nationalgeographic.com/kids/places/ find/china/>